WHOSOEVER

Revealing the Riches
of
John 3:16

§

by
Jerry Vines

To Kimberly

Jerry Vines

WHOSOEVER—Revealing the Riches of John 3:16
by Dr. Jerry Vines

ISBN: 9781939283061

Unless otherwise indicated, all Scripture taken from the King James Version of the Holy Bible. All Greek text translations are the author's.

Scripture quotations marked (NASB) are taken from the *New American Standard Bible*®, Copyright © 1960, 1962, 1963, 1971, 1972, 1973, 1975, 1977, 1995 by The Lockman Foundation. Used by permission.

Printed in the United States of America by Lightning Source, Inc.
Cover Design: Jessica Anglea www.jessicaanglea.com
Text design by Debbie Patrick, Vision Run, www.visionrun.com

Free Church Press
P.O. Box 1075
Carrollton, GA 30112

Contents

Preface

§

In 2007 I spent a year studying one single verse in the Bible. I was getting ready for the first "John 3:16 Conference" which was held in 2008 at First Baptist Church, Woodstock, Georgia. My year's study was in preparation for the opening message of the conference. The verse? John 3:16. I cannot tell you how blessed I was to consider that glorious verse word by word. I became convinced that it is indeed the greatest verse in the Bible. Therein we find the mind of God, the heart of God and the will of God as it relates to the salvation of mankind.

Since that time I have continued to study John 3:16. In 2013 I preached the opening of our second "John 3:16 Conference" held at North Metro Baptist Church, Lawrenceville, Georgia. I preached a message entitled "For Whose Sins Did Jesus Die?" In preparation for that message I continued my study of John 3:16 along with some other pertinent passages. I found many more precious tokens of God's love for fallen mankind. Every time I study it I find new avenues of thought and new assurances to any person who wants to be saved.

This small book tries to put together much of the material I have gathered on John 3:16. Of course, I do not claim in any way that I have exhausted the explanation and meaning of the verse. I am just sharing with you the results of my continuing study.

In this book I have included some technical study of the Greek text of John 3:16. If you are not a student of the Greek language, do not let this hinder you from getting the blessings of this marvelous verse. If need be, just skip over the technical parts (for convenience of English readers, following each Greek word is included an English transliteration of the Greek text in brackets).

Also, I have sought to share sermonic material I have used in preaching this verse through the years of my ministry. There are explanations, applications, and illustrations I believe will be helpful to you.

In the 2009 BCS championship game between Florida and Ohio State, Florida's Quarterback Tim Tebow wore John 3:16 on his eye black. In the next 24 hours John 3:16 was the highest-ranked Google search, generating 90,300,000 searches. Only heaven will reveal how many people came to Christ as a result of finding and acting upon that verse! Who can imagine how many people have been saved through that verse since John, inspired by the Holy Spirit, recorded it in his Gospel. I believe any witness can lead a person to Christ with John 3:16.

I pray those who desire to win the lost to Christ will find helpful information here. Most of all, I pray my book will find its way into the hands of multitudes who do not know Christ, read it, and come to the Lord Jesus for salvation.

Now, go with me as we enjoy *Whosoever: Revealing the Riches of John 3:16!*

Jerry Vines, Pastor–Emeritus,
First Baptist Church, Jacksonville, Florida;
two time President, Southern Baptist Convention;
President, Jerry Vines Ministries, Inc.

Introduction

In the 1870s archaeologists uncovered in the sands of Egypt a giant, red granite obelisk. They quickly named it "Cleopatra's Needle," and gave it to London (Three obelisks were actually found. Egypt gave them to Paris, New York, and London). This 68-foot high shaft was erected in London on the banks of the Thames River. At the base of the shaft a time vault was placed. Several items of the times were included in the vault: some coins and clothing; children's toys; a newspaper; pictures of the 12 prettiest women in London. A committee was appointed to include the greatest single verse in the Bible. The committee was unanimous. In the 220 known languages of the time, the verse placed in the time vault was John 3:16.

John 3:16 is probably the best known verse in the Bible. Perhaps it is the first verse we learn and the last one we forget. Multitudes have been led to faith in Christ by this one verse.

Herschel Hobbs called it "the Gospel in superlatives." For Martin Luther, it was "the Bible in Miniature." A.T. Robertson referred to it as "the Little Gospel." Others have called it "the Mount Everest of Holy Scripture," and "the most exquisite flower in the Garden of Holy Scripture." The one I like best is "the Gospel in a nutshell." If all the other verses in the Bible were lost and this one remained, all the rest of the Bible is contained in this one verse. There is enough Gospel truth in this single verse to lead "Whosoever" to faith in Christ.

John 3:16 addresses a number of "-isms" that ought to become "-wasms." That is, they need to be *past* tense! "For God …" answers ATHE<u>ISM</u>, which says there is no God; "so loved …" answers FATAL<u>ISM</u>, which says God is an impersonal force; "the world …" answers NATIONAL<u>ISM</u>, which says God loves only one people group; "that He gave …" answers MATERIAL<u>ISM</u>, which says it is more blessed to receive than to give; "His only begotten Son …" answers MUHAMMAD<u>ISM</u>, which says God did not have a Son; "that whosoever believes … answers CALVIN<u>ISM</u>, which says Christ died only for the elect; "in Him …" answers PLURAL<u>ISM</u>, which says all religions are equally the same; "should not perish …" answers ANNIHILATION<u>ISM</u>, which says there is no hell; "but have everlasting life" answers ARMINIAN<u>ISM</u>, which says God gives only conditional life. John 3:16 is a simple Biblicism which reveals the mind, the heart and the will of God concerning His love for human kind and His desire that "whosoever" might be saved.

F.W. Boreham called it everybody's text. Here is a verse so profound, all the scholars of all the ages could never plumb its depths. Yet, a verse so simple, a little child in Sunday School can understand its meaning. Perhaps more people have come to faith in Christ by this verse than any other. John 3:16 is a verse for people who are, who were and who are yet to be.

This single verse may also be called the inexhaustible text. The great evangelist D.L. Moody met a young preacher in England named Henry Moorhead. Moody told young Moorhead that should he ever come to America, he would ask him to preach at his church in Chicago. To his great surprise, he soon received a telegram saying, "I have landed in New York, and I will be coming to Chicago to preach for you." Moody was to be away on a trip and instructed that the young man should preach one night. Upon his return he was again surprised that young Moorhead had preached several nights with growing crowds and many coming to Christ. Moody's wife said to him, "He's a better preacher than you. He preaches that God loves people." And, he was told that Moorhead had preached every night from John 3:16. Now, here's where the story gets really interesting. Moorhead started preaching at 16; he died an untimely death at 33. His text for every sermon was John 3:16. The messages were different, but the text was the same. Surely no preacher in a lifetime could ever exhaust this text.

This verse is inexhaustible because it is about the love of God. I have given myself an impossible assignment in this little book. I will attempt to expound John 3:16. But, who can fully expound the love of God? The noted British painter William Morris was to paint the portrait of the gorgeous Jane Burden. After quite a while Morris wrote on the canvas and turned it to Burden. He had written, "I can't paint you, but I love you." Such is our feeling when we contemplate the love of God as revealed in John 3:16. The Gospel song has captured the dilemma I face:

Could we with ink the ocean fill,
and were the skies of parchment made.

Were every stalk on earth a quill,
and every man a scribe by trade.
To write the love of God above.
would drain the ocean dry.
Nor could the scroll contain the whole,
though stretched from sky to sky.

Perhaps John 3:16 has become slick from frequent usage. If we aren't careful, it will roll off our mind without lodging. I certainly do not approach it casually or with a sense of competency. I identify with the spirit of A.W. Tozer who said, "I think my own hesitation to preach from John 3:16 comes down to this: I appreciate it so profoundly that I am frightened by it—I am overwhelmed by John 3:16 to the point of inadequacy, almost of despair. Along with this is my knowledge that if a minister is to try to preach John 3:16, he must be endowed with great sympathy and a genuine love for God and man ... so I approach it as one who is filled with great fear and yet great fascination. I take off my shoes, my heart shoes, at least, as I come to this declaration that God so loved the world"(A. W. Tozer, *Christ the Eternal Son*, Christian Publications, pp. 85-86).

I want to examine this marvelous verse in some detail. Hopefully I will not destroy its beauty as one would a flower in over-analyzing its parts. I will attempt to examine the Greek text in some detail. This should not hinder the reader unversed in Greek from drawing an understanding of the meaning of the verse. I also attempt to approach the verse without imposing my own theological assumptions upon it. I am aware that none of us can completely avoid bringing our theological presuppositions to bear upon Scripture. But, I agree with Dr. David Allen who says, "Exegesis must precede systematic theology as well as historic theology" (*Whosoever Will*, Nashville: Broadman and Holman Academic, p. 78). To be sure I am interested in what systematic theology and Christian history have to say. There is much to be learned from both fields of study. But, ultimately, I want to know what does my inerrant Bible say? For Bible believing people this will settle the matter. Jesus said, "Search the Scriptures; for in them ye think ye have eternal life: and they are they which testify of Me."(John 5:39). From John 3:16 I want to make several statements about God's love.

Chapter One

GOD'S LOVE IS GLOBAL
"For God so loved the world."

ORIGIN

This opening phrase tells us of the origin of this love. "God." When I was a teenager a group of us decided to trace a stream to its source. It was not easy. After going quite a distance, through a great deal of underbrush, ditches and thickets, we finally found a beautiful spring. John 3:16 begins its explanation of love by tracing it to its origin— the heart of God Himself. The word for God in the Greek text is θεός (*theos*) and is singular. There are not many gods. There is only one God. There is no attempt here, nor anywhere in the Bible, to prove the existence of God. The Bible begins, "In the beginning God …"(Genesis 1:1). Some truths are self-evident or innate. We just know them to be truthful. There is a renewed effort on the part of the atheist community to deny the existence of God. Christopher Hutchins' book, *God Is Not Great*, and Richard Dawkins', *The God Delusion* loudly proclaim the same old tired arguments attempting to disprove God's existence. Someone said the atheists have complained that Christians have all the special days: Christmas; Easter; the Lord's Day. They want one. Ok. I would suggest April 1. Psalm 14:1 says, "The fool hath said in his heart, 'there is no God'." Belief in the existence of God is the fundamental postulate of all rational thinking.

The Greek text places a definite article before θεός (*theos*). The article gives emphasis and definiteness. Not just any God, but "THE God." The reference is to the only God there is. Not just one among many other gods. The God of love is the only God there is! Of course, in the New Testament day people believed in many gods. According to 1 Corinthians 10:20-21 those so-called gods were non-existent. There were demons behind them. The other gods of today's religions are in the same category. Allah and Buddha do not exist. The only God there is is the God of the Bible!

> **Allah and Buddha do not exist. The only God there is is the God of the Bible!**

But, the ancients believed in all kinds of gods. They had gods galore. They had peaceful gods and fighting gods. They had lazy gods and lustful gods. There were all kinds of gods. It was "here a god, there a god, everywhere a god, a god." But, Jesus came talking about the God who was different. Never would it have occurred to people of that time that their gods were capable of love. John 3:16 makes an assertion that was absolutely revolutionary at the time: God is a God of love. To be sure God is *omnipresent* (He is everywhere); *omniscient* (He is all knowing); and *omnipotent* (He is all powerful). But, the fundamental assertion about God is that he is *omnibenevolent* (He is all loving).

In his First Epistle John declares, "God is love" (1 John 4:8). This truth can utterly capture your heart. D. L. Moody had a gas sign at the front of his Moody Tabernacle that read, "God is love." One night a man came to Christ in the service. "What was it about the service that brought you to Christ?" asked Moody. "Was it the singing?" "Oh, the singing was glorious, but that wasn't it." "Well, was it my message?" Moody inquired. "Your message was fine, but that wasn't it." "What was it then?" curious Moody queried. The man said, "It was that sign—'God is love' that did it."

Indeed, a love that originates in the heart of God has a magnificent drawing power. 1 John 3:1 says, "Behold what manner of love the Father hath bestowed upon us …" The word ποταπός (*potapós*, translated "manner" in the English Bible) literally means, from what country? John 3:16 tells us about a love that is literally out of this world! Not of this country! A love that originates in heaven; yes, even in the heart of God! So, what is our take away from this opening phrase? There is Someone who loves you—The God of the universe.

Many years ago now I was preaching on the love of God. During the invitation time a college age girl came forward. She took my hand, looked into my eyes, and said, "Are you telling me that God really loves me?" I answered, that, yes indeed, God loved her. Tears welled up in her eyes as she seemed to grasp for the first time that she was loved by God. There are many people who wonder if anyone loves them; if anyone cares; if anyone is seeking them. John 3:16 declares that there is a God who loves us all.

OVERFLOW

The phrase also tells us about the overflow of this love. "So loved." Let's look for a moment at the verb—"loved" [ἀγαπάω (*agapáō*)]. This is the load-bearing verb in the verse. The verb is placed in the dominant position in the text. Literally it is, "so loved the God …"

We use the word, love, in so many ways today. "I love my wife." "I love peanut butter and jelly sandwiches." "I love football." The word for love here is very special.

There were three main Greek words for love. One is ἐρᾶν (*eros*). We get our word, erotic from it. This is a word that describes a desire only to take. I call this SENSUAL love. So odious is this word it is not planted one time in the sweet soil of Scripture. Another is φίλον (*philos*). We get our word, Philadelphia from that word (the city of brotherly love). This word conveys the idea of affection or friendship. The word describes a reciprocal give and take kind of love. I call this SOCIAL love. The word used here is ἀγαπάω (*agape*). This word indicates a love to the highest degree. The idea is a love that desires to give, based on the character of the one loving, not upon the worthiness of the one who is loved. The author of this Gospel, the apostle John, is known as the "disciple Jesus loved." John seems not to be able to fathom such love, for he uses it 36 times in his book. This is SPIRITUAL love.

Let me get a bit technical here. The verb translated "loved" is ἀγαπάω (*agapáō*), a first aorist indicative active verb. Greek scholars say it is a constantive aorist. Not an ingressive aorist, indicating there was a time when God *began to love* us. Not a cumulative aorist, indicating there will be a time when God will *cease to love* us. But, a constantive aorist, emphasizing God's *constant, total, eternal love*; God's love in its entirety.

What God says in Jeremiah 31:3 helps us get a glimpse into such total, eternal love. There He says, "Yea, I have loved thee with an everlasting love …" The Hebrew word for "everlasting" means "beyond vanishing point." A teenager might put it this way—God's love is out of sight!

God's love extends into eternity past. This means there was never a time when God began to love you. My wife, Janet, told all our grandchildren, "I loved you before you were born." Our granddaughter, Ashlyn, was visiting us when she was a little girl. She jumped on the bed with Mema, cupped her hands under her chin and said, "Mema, I loved you before you were born!" There was a time when you began to love your mate or your children. There was never a time when God began to love you. Before you were born, before the world was created or the sun and moon and stars existed, God loved you.

God's love reaches to eternity future. There will never be a time when God will cease to love you. When you are no longer on the earth, when the earth quits spinning on its axis, when the heavens roll away like a scroll and the stars fall from their sockets like chunks of coal, God will still love you.

There is nothing you can do that will cause God not to love you. A couple engaged a baby sitter to care for their young daughter so they could have a night out. When they returned and the baby sitter left, the little girl began to whimper. "What's the matter, dear?" asked her parents. "Beth told me if I misbehaved, you wouldn't love me." The couple held her in their arms and assured her they would love her regardless. *Jesus loves me when I'm good, when I do the things I should. Jesus loves me when I'm bad, though it makes Him very sad.*

Now, let's spend a little time with the adverb "so." A study of various Greek lexicons conveys the idea that this is a qualitative and a quantitative adverb. BDAG (short for *The Bauer-Danker Lexicon,* among the most respected Greek lexicons available) indicates it is a demonstrative adverb. Thus, the word could be translated "in this manner," or "to this degree." Thayer's Lexicon calls it an adverb of degree. This would render the translation, "to such an infinite degree" or "in such a glorious manner." The McArthur Study Bible says that "so" emphasizes the intensity or greatness of God's love. Perhaps we may combine both ideas by translating it "God loved the world in such an intense manner."

"So!" There are volumes in that little word. God's love is not like a trickling stream; it's like a flooding river. "So!" His love is not like a leaky faucet; it's like a bottomless ocean. "So!" The love of God is not like a flickering lightning bug; it's like a blinding sun. A few summers ago Lake Lanier and Lake Allatoona, near where we live, were dangerously low. There was talk of having to restrict water use. Not so God's love. His love is an eternal reservoir that never runs dry!

Napoleon's soldiers opened a dungeon and found a skeleton in the prison. The prisoner had evidently cut a cross on the wall, with Ephesians 3:18-19 written underneath. The passage speaks of the "breadth, length, height and depth" of God's love. The cross reminds us that God's love is so wide it includes all sinners everywhere; so long, it stretches from eternity to the farthest sinner; so deep, it stoops to the lowest sinner; and so high, it can carry every sinner to heaven!

OBJECT

The last word in the phrase tells us of the object of this love—"the world." The Greek word κόσμος (*kosmos*) is fairly familiar—*cosmos*. Here, it is an accusative singular, the direct object of the verb, "loved." We get our word, cosmetics from it. The idea is to arrange or put in order. John likes the word (His writings include over half the 185 occurrences in the New Testament: 78 times in his Gospel; 24 in his epistles). He uses it with a few different meanings. Sometimes cosmos refers to the world as the *physical universe* (cp. 1:9, 10; 17:5). A few times it speaks of the *evil world system* that arranges itself in hostility to God (cp. John 17:6, 14, 16; etc.). Overwhelmingly, John uses the word to refer to the *people* who live in the physical realm. A. T. Robertson was perhaps the greatest Greek scholar of all time. He says that here John means "the whole human race."(A. T. Robertson, *Word Pictures in the Greek New Testament*, vol. 5, Nashville: Broadman, p.50). Here the word indicates, not the world of nature, nor the world system, but the *sum total of all people*.

Before we look in more detail at "world," let us consider those verses that say Christ gave His life for "many." Does this indicate that God just loves many and not all? Did Christ die for just many and not all? For our purposes, consider two references:

- "Even as the Son of Man came not to be minis-
  tered unto, but to minister, and to give his life a
  ransom for many"(Matt. 20:28).

- "... For if through the offence of one many be
  dead, much more the grace of God, and the gift
  by grace, which is by One man, Jesus Christ, hath
  abounded unto many"(Rom. 5:15).

What do we make of statements like these? Do they mean
God did not love nor give His Son for the world but only a
few? To understand the contrast intended leads us to a correct
interpretation. The contrast is not "many" in contrast to "all."
Rather, the contrast is "many" in contrast to "few." The verses
aren't saying Christ died for many but not for all. They mean
Christ died for many not just a few. Romans 5:19 says, "For as
by one man's disobedience many were made sinners, so by the
obedience of One shall many be made righteous." "Many" here
clearly means "all," for all are sinners (cp. Romans 3:23). First
Timothy 2:6 settles the matter, "Who (Christ) gave himself a
ransom for ALL, to be testified in due time."

In John's Gospel "the world" *never* means the world of the
elect. Actually John places the elect in contrast to the world
in 17:6, "I have manifested thy name unto the men which
Thou gavest me (the elect) out of the world (of humanity)."
To be sure God does love the elect and Christ did die for
them. "He that spared not his own Son, but delivered him
up for us all, how shall he not with him also freely give us all
things? Who shall lay any thing to the charge of God's elect?
It is God that justifieth."(Rom. 8:32-33); "Elect according to
the foreknowledge of God the Father, through sanctification
of the Spirit, unto obedience and sprinkling of the blood of

22

Jesus Christ …" (1 Pet. 1:2). But Scripture never isolates the elect and says God loves only them or that Christ died only for them. First John 2:2 is decisive, "And He is the propitiation for our sins (the elect); and not for ours only, but also for the sins of the whole world (the world of humanity)."

> Scripture never isolates the elect and says God loves only them or that Christ died only for them.

Let's spend a few minutes with Galatians 2:20, "I am crucified with Christ: nevertheless I live; yet not I, but Christ liveth in me: and the life which I now live in the flesh I live by the faith of the Son of God, who loved me, and gave Himself for me." How thrilling to know that God loves me and that Christ died for me individually. Several Biblical terms identify what kind of person I am for whom Christ died. He died for SINNERS, "But God commendeth His love toward us, in that, while we were yet sinners, Christ died for us"(Rom. 5:8). "This is a faithful saying, and worthy of all acceptation, that Christ Jesus came into the world to save sinners; of whom I am chief"(1 Tim. 1:15). Sinners? That's me! He died for THE UNGODLY, "For when we were yet without strength, in due time Christ died for the ungodly."(Rom. 5:6). Ungodly? That's me! He died for THE UNJUST, "For Christ also hath once suffered for sins, the just for the unjust …"(1 Pet. 3:18). Unjust? That's me! But, to say that Christ loves me and gave Himself for me, does that mean He loves only me and no one else? A logical fallacy is involved that we will explore later.

Think for a moment about Ephesians 5:25, "... Christ also loved the church and gave Himself for it." Does that mean He loves only the church (the congregation of believers) and no one else? There are several terms that seem to be synonymous with the word "church." Christ Jesus gave Himself for THE FLOCK, "Take heed therefore unto yourselves, and to all the flock, over the which the Holy Ghost hath made you overseers, to feed the church of God, which He hath purchased with His own blood" (Acts 20:28). Does this mean He loves only the flock? Christ also gave Himself for HIS SHEEP, "I am the good Shepherd; the good Shepherd giveth His life for the sheep ... I lay down my life for the sheep" (John 10:11, 15). Did Christ die only for His sheep? He gave Himself for HIS PEOPLE, "He hath visited and redeemed his people"(Luke 1:68); "Thou shalt call his name Jesus: for he shall save his people from their sins"(Matt. 1:21). Does that mean He loved only His people? The Lord gave Himself for the NATION, "... he (Caiphas) prophesied that Jesus should die for that nation" (John 11:51). Did He die only for His nation Israel? He died for HIS FRIENDS, "Greater love hath no man than this, that a man lay down his life for his friends" (John 15:13). Were His friends the only ones who were the objects of His love?

To say when Scripture says Christ died for His church, His flock or His sheep, His people or nation or His friends that it means He died ONLY for me and them and did not die for the world is a logical fallacy. For me to say I love my wife and children certainly does not mean I love only them and do not love many friends, and yes, the whole world.

Surely the Bible is clear that God loves all the people of the world. To say otherwise seems to slander the love of God.

If God doesn't love all the people of the world, why did He create them?

The fact remains, God loves all the people of the world. God doesn't just love Christians; He loves all people. He doesn't love just Americans; He loves all nations. He doesn't love just the white people; He loves all races. Is there any boy or girl anywhere in the world who cannot truthfully sing, "Jesus loves the little children, all the children of the world. Red and yellow, black and white, they are precious in His sight. Jesus loves the little children of the world"?

This is an incredible truth in light of the vastness of the universe. Our sun is 93 million miles from the earth. Boarding a space car, at 150mph we could get there in 70 years. Taking a jet, at 600mph we would arrive in 17 years. Why would God love such an infinitesimally small planet as ours? Psalm 8:3-4 raises that question, "When I consider thy heavens, the work of thy fingers the moon and the stars, which thou hast ordained, what is man that thou art mindful of him? And the son of man, that thou visitest him?"

Unbelief would say that God doesn't care about us. Carl Sagan said, "Our planet is a lonely speck in the great enveloping cosmic dark. In our obscurity, in all this vastness, there is no hint that help will come from elsewhere to save us from ourselves" (Quoted by Max Lucado). But, John 3:16 shouts that God does care! As I write today there are 7.1 billion people in the world. Put them all in a line passing before God. He would say to each one, "I love you, Bill; I love you, Mary; I love you, Omar; I love you, Aalia; I love you, Jose." God loves each and every one of the people in the whole world. This is an incredible truth in light of the lostness of humanity.

What kind of people are loved by God? We learn the answer to this from the Bible. 1 John 5:19 declares, "The whole world lies in wickedness (or, the wicked one)." The world of humanity is like a precious vessel sunk in a putrid stream of depravity. Romans 3:19 says that the entire world is guilty before God.

We also learn from observation. Look without. Daily news of the atrocities people commit against one another drives home the fallenness of the human race. A drunken father burns off the fingers of his little child. A live-in boyfriend rapes his girl friend's 6 month old baby, giving it AIDS. Terrorists kill hundreds in savage bombings. A man abducts three girls, keeps them a decade, beating them, impregnating them, and subjecting them to unimaginable horrors. How could God love people like that? Remember, God's love is not conditioned on the worthiness of the object, but upon the character of the God who is love (1 John 4:8).

Looking within our own hearts, to think God loves us is incredible. Jeremiah 17:9 says, "The heart is deceitful above all things, and desperately wicked: who can know it?" To see the depths of my own sin and shame makes it truly amazing that God loves the world. My great mentor, Evangelist Jess Hendley, used to say, "Only God could love a human being."

Move this truth closer to you. Ephesians 5:25 says, "Christ loved the church and gave himself for it." If you are a believer in Christ, you are part of His church. His love for you is evidenced by the fact that He gave Himself for the church.

Move this truth still closer. Galatians 2:20 teaches that the Son of God "loved me, and gave himself for me." I remember well the song we used to sing in my boyhood church. *I am so glad that our Father in heaven tells of His love in the Book He has given. Wonderful things in the Bible I see. This is the dearest, that Jesus loves me.* I can still feel the thrill in my soul as I sang the refrain at the top of my voice, *I am so glad that Jesus loves me, Jesus loves me, Jesus loves me. I am so glad that Jesus loves me, Jesus loves even me.* Every little boy and girl in the world can truthfully and correctly sing that song.

God's love is not conditioned on the worthiness of the object, but upon the character of the God who is love.

Do you remember one of the first songs we ever learned in Sunday School? *Jesus loves me, this I know, for the Bible tells me so. Little ones to Him belong, we are weak, but He is strong. Yes, Jesus loves me. Yes, Jesus loves me. Yes, Jesus loves me, for the Bible tells me so.* Though some have doubted its truthfulness, the following story has been verified by some who were present and one biographer. When at Union Theological Seminary, the great theologian Karl Barth was asked by a reporter to summarize his *Church Dogmatics.* Barth thought for a moment and then said, "Jesus loves me this I know, for the Bible tells me so." And it is so!

Augustine said, "God loves each one of us as if there was only one of us to love." How can God love each and every one of the 7.1 billion people in the world individually? I have a pastor friend who said a woman in his church taught him an important truth about God's love for each of us. She had 10 children. He asked her, "You have so many children, do you ever neglect any of them?" The mother replied, "Oh no, I never forget a one of them, 'cause they're all precious to me." My pastor friend learned something about a mother's heart. A mother's heart doesn't operate by the laws of division—one mother's heart divided 10 ways. A mother's heart operates by the laws of multiplication—one mother's heart multiplied 10 ways. Extrapolate that to God's heart. His heart doesn't operate by the laws of division—one heart divided 7.1 billion ways. God's heart operates by the laws of multiplication—one Father's heart multiplied 7.1 billion ways!

There is a world out there that needs to know God loves them. Wherever you go, whomever you see or meet, remember, this is a person loved by God. Why do we have churches? "For God so loved the world." Why do we preach? "For God so loved the world." Why do we witness? "For God so loved the world." Why do we send missionaries? "For God so loved the world."

Bennett Cerf, founder of Random House Publishing, told a moving story. There was a child in a Children's Home who was somewhat troublesome and difficult. The workers of the home were looking for an excuse to move the unwanted child to another Home. One day the child was seen stealing across the grounds to a tree. Climbing up the tree she deposited a note in one of the branches. When the child was gone the workers rushed to the tree and retrieved the note. They opened it up, and it read, "If anybody finds this, I love you." Our world treats God like an unwanted child in a Children's Home. To a world that doesn't love Him, God says in John 3:16, "If anyone finds this, I love you."

Chapter Two

GOD'S LOVE IS SACRIFICIAL
"That He gave His only begotten Son"

§

The next phrase of John 3:16 begins with the word ὥστε (*hoste*), a word translated in the English Bible as "that." This is the translation of a consecutive conjunction introducing a result clause. The indication is that God loved the world to such an intense degree it resulted in Him giving His Son. God loved; He gave. Love always gives. The nature of fire is to burn. Light's nature is to shine. Love's nature is to give (see Ephesians 5:25; Galatians 2:20). One may give but not love. But one may not love and not give. So much of what we hear called love today is not really love but lust. Much so-called "love" today is about taking, not giving. The idea is "I love me and I want you to give to me."

Love is a noun (1 John 4:8). But love is also a verb. Love is a decision. To be sure, there is emotion involved in love. Remember when you had your first puppy love? Your emotions were excited; your heart throbbed; you were "falling in love." By the way, watch out for "puppy love," it can lead to a dog's life! I used to quote this little poem to my church young people:

Love's a very funny thing
it's shaped just like a lizard.
It wraps its tail around your throat,
and goes right through your gizzard.

Love is primarily a decision. You decided to love your mate. You decided to love your husband, not realizing his hair would fall out, he would snore at night, and his teeth would have to be replaced. You decided to love your wife, never thinking she would bite her toenails and eat peanut butter in bed. You decided to love your spouse, in spite of all the irritating traits and emotional baggage he/she would bring into the relationship.

Love always demonstrates itself. A boy wrote his girlfriend a love letter: "I love you so much I would climb the highest mountain for you. I would swim the deepest river, go through snow and hail for you. P.S. And if it doesn't rain Friday night, I'll be over to see you." When God sent His Son He demonstrated His love for the world. Hallmark Cards has the slogan, "When you care enough to send the very best." God decided to send His very best, His only begotten Son.

DEFINITELY

God gave His Son *definitely*. "Gave." God made a decision to give His Son. This phrase is loaded with Gospel meaning. The Greek word is δίδωμι (*dídōmi*). God loves us so very much He gave His Son definitely. The verb translated "gave" is a third person singular aorist indicative in the Greek text. The aorist is another constantive, indicating the totality and definiteness of His act of giving His Son. 1 John 4:10 says, "Herein is love, not that we loved God, but that he loved us, and sent his

Son to be the propitiation for our sins." ἀποστέλλω (*apostéllō,* and translated "sent" in the KJV) is another aorist tense verb, indicating God's definite decision. The particular Greek word used here means to "send off or away" on a mission. Included in that word is the incarnation, crucifixion, resurrection and exaltation of our Lord Jesus. God sent His Son tenderly, wonderfully, lovingly, definitely.

I sometimes imagine that God, knowing mankind would sin and need a Savior, surveyed the farthest reaches of heaven. He looked for someone to send to earth to be the Savior. He surveyed all the cherubim and seraphim. None of them would do. He looked at the archangels and angels. None was good enough. Then His holy gaze fell upon His darling Son. In the counsels of the Godhead it was agreed that the Son would come to be the Savior of the world.

Imagine how it was when the Lord left heaven. As He exited the gates of glory the angels cry, "Don't go down there Jesus; they will misunderstand and mistreat you." But down He came. As He passed by, Jupiter cried, "Don't go down there Jesus; they will slap you and beat you and spit on you." But down, down He came. He goes by the sun and the sun cries out, "Don't go down there Jesus; they will ram a spear in your side, crush a crown of thorns on your head and drive nails into your hands." But, down, down, down He came.

He came all the way from the glory place to the gory place. What a journey it was! *Out of the ivory palaces, into a world of woe. Only His great, eternal love, made our Savior go.* He came down to this godless globe, to be born in a smelly manger, live in a hick town, work as a carpenter, be rejected by His own and be nailed to a cross.

Why did God do it? "In this was manifested the love of God toward us, because that God sent His only begotten Son into the world, that we might live through Him."(1 John 4:9). God gave Him definitely.

UNIQUELY

> He came down to this godless globe, to be born in a smelly manger, live in a hick town, work as a carpenter, be rejected by His own and be nailed to a cross.

God gave His Son *uniquely.* The Greek phrase is υἱὸν τὸν μονογενῆ (*huion ho monogenḗs*)—"His only begotten." *Monogenḗs* comes from a compound Greek word, made up of two Greek words. *Mono* means "only." We get words like monorail and monopoly from it. *Genes* means kind or offspring. We get our words, gene and genetics, from it. Those two words are combined to translate our word as "only begotten."

The word is an adjective used in several other places. The widow's son was her only begotten (Luke 7:12). Jairus' daughter was his only begotten (Luke 9:38). Isaac is referred to as Abraham's only begotten (Hebrews 11:17). Abraham had another son, Ishmael. But Isaac was Abraham's "only begotten son" in the sense that he was born in a miraculous manner. Jesus was God's Son in a sense no one else can ever be.

John actually uses it to refer to Christ five times (Here; John 1:14, 18; 3:18 and 1 John 4:9). As used in John 3:16 it modifies the noun "Son." The word conveys the uniqueness of Christ. Only Jesus has God's genes. The Son's eternal relationship to the Father is highlighted. Jesus was God's Son in a sense no one else can ever be.

Clearly implied is the absolute deity of Jesus Christ. When Jesus was born, He was uniquely born. He was virgin born! Think about the uniqueness of our Lord's virgin birth.

There is a mystery about His birth. When I was pastor of Dauphin Way Baptist Church in Mobile, Alabama, a noted gynecologist, Dr. Mitchell, was a member. At that time he had delivered over 16,000 babies! I used to take him to lunch and ask him to explain biological birth to me. He would do so with long, technical words. I would sit there and act like I understood them! After he would finish his explanation, we would look at one another, aware that, when considering biological birth, you are in the presence of a miracle.

But, none was ever born as Jesus was. First Timothy 3:16 begins, "Without controversy, great is the mystery of godliness: God was manifest in the flesh ..." Think about it. When Jesus was born God was born. The Infinite became an infant. The Creator became a creature. God cuddled in a cradle. Who can understand that?! The eternal God confined Himself to the narrow dimensions of a woman's womb; He restricted Himself to a single sperm cell. R. G. Lee used to say Jesus was the only One ever born who had a heavenly Father, but no heavenly mother; an earthly mother, but no earthly father. He was the only One ever born who was older than His mother and as old as His Father!

Jesus said on one occasion, "Before Abraham was, I am" (John 8:58). What a mystery!

There is a must about His birth. Liberalism says it doesn't matter whether Jesus was virgin born or not. Does the virgin birth not matter? Absolutely essential is His virgin birth. Had Jesus not been virgin born, He could not have lived a sinless life. No sinless life, no perfect sacrifice at the cross for the sins of the world. No perfect sacrifice, then no salvation available for us.

> **By means of the virgin birth God short-circuited the sin cycle, so that Jesus was never tainted by original sin.**

By means of the virgin birth God short-circuited the sin cycle, so that Jesus was never tainted by original sin. The same Holy Spirit who impregnated the earth and brought forth beauty impregnated the womb of Mary and brought forth Deity. Dr. Luke, considering the virgin birth of our Lord, records what the angel Gabriel said to the virgin Mary, "The Holy Ghost shall come upon thee, and the power of the Highest shall overshadow thee: therefore also that holy thing which shall be born of thee shall be called the Son of God"(Luke 1:35). Jesus is the only One ever born who could be referred to as "that holy thing." I know we all love our children. But, could we ever refer to any of them as "that holy thing?" I guarantee you when he/she lets out that unholy scream in a temper tantrum in the middle of the night, you don't refer to him/her as "that holy thing!" His sinlessness qualified Him to be the perfect atonement for our sins.

There is magnificence about His birth. How different it would have been if slick Madison Avenue marketing experts had planned it. They would have had Him born to a stylish model in a Trump Towers Condo; God had Him born to a humble Jewish girl. They would have placed Him on the soft, satin pillows of a king's palace; God placed Him on the coarse straw of a smelly animal stable. They would have announced His birth to scholars; God announced Him to common shepherds. Yet, wise men came to worship Him, a king feared Him, angels praised Him and the Father was pleased with Him! Magnificent indeed.

INCREDIBLY

God gave His Son *incredibly*. The word order and the use of the definite article in the phrase are significant. Literally the Greek text translates, "The Son the only begotten He gave." John is calling attention to the incredible truth that it was His only Son, His unique Son that He gave. Romans 8:32 uses a strengthened form of the word "gave", "He that spared not His own Son, but delivered Him up for us all …" He gave Him up. The idea of sacrifice is indicated by this word. In the word we hear echoes of Abraham's willingness to sacrifice His Son, Isaac (Genesis 22). God not only gave His Son to the world, He gave Him up to the world. Oh, to what He gave Him up!

God gave Him up to scourging. I never really understood the severity of scourging until I saw the TV movie series *Roots* and saw the scourging of Toby. The depiction of our Lord's scourging in *The Passion of the Christ* brought home its severity to me again. A normal Jewish scourging was to be 39 stripes,

13 on each shoulder and 13 on the small of the back. This was to ensure that the Biblical mandate was not exceeded, "Forty stripes he may give him, and not exceed ..."(Deuteronomy 25:3). But, Jesus was beaten with the Roman halfway death. So severe was this scourging that men went raving mad under it; some died. All of this was prophesied. "I gave my back to the smiters" (Isa. 50:6); "the plowers plowed my back; they made deep their furrows"(Psa. 129:3).

This scourging was administered by a Roman Lictor, a soldier trained in the brutal art of scourging. He used a flagellum, which was a piece of wood with strips of leather. Attached to the strips were pieces of polished bone and steel. In the hands of the Lictor it became a whistling monster. Can you hear the ripping of our Lord's flesh? Do you see the splattering of His blood, His exposed, quivering veins? That's what the Father gave Him up to.

God gave Him up to crucifixion. Death by crucifixion was the cruelest punishment ever devised by the depraved minds of men. Some say the Phoenicians got the idea for it from seeing rats nailed to a wall. They drove Jesus to Calvary. There on 'ole skull hill, amid the screaming and the spitting, the filth and the gore, they lay the bruised, battered body of the Lord. They nail Him to the cross, then lift Him between heaven and earth as if He is fit for neither. We hear the dull thud as the cross drops into the hole prepared. We hear the flesh rip and the lungs heave. Jesus' muscles pull, His bones disjoint, His tendons shred, His heart pumps desperately. His every movement sends pain, with shoes of fire, racing up and down His nervous system. Oriental insects feast on His body. The hot oriental sun beats down upon

Him, drying up the mucous membrane, so that every time He swallows it is like chunks of granite tearing His throat. Oh what physical misery he suffered.

There is more. He also endured spiritual misery on the cross. Martin Luther was said to have spent hours contemplating the words of Jesus when He said, "My God, my God, why hast thou forsaken me?"(Matt. 27:46). Then he was heard to exclaim, "God forsaken of God, who can understand that?!"The songwriter expressed it aptly, *But none of the ransomed ever knew how deep were the waters crossed. Nor how dark was the night that the Lord passed through 'ere He found His sheep that were lost.*

Why did He suffer such physical and spiritual misery? For what was Jesus dying? Scripture makes it very clear. He was dying for our sins. He was making the sacrifice for the sins of the world. 1 Cor. 15:3 says, "He died for our sins." Gal. 1:4 declares, "who (Christ) gave Himself for our sins …" 1 John 2:2 couldn't be clearer, "He is the propitiation for our sins: and not for ours only, but also the sins of the whole world." Some might die for a family member or a friend. Jesus died for sinners (Romans 5:8), the ungodly (Romans 5:6), the unjust (1 Peter 3:18), for me (Gal. 2:20), and for every person (Heb. 2:9).

The sacrificial gift of God's Son places God's love beyond all doubt. Our hearts can sing, *What wondrous love is this, O my soul … that caused the Lord of bliss to bear the dreadful curse, for my soul.* God does not love us because Christ died; Christ died because God loves us. Romans 5:8 says, "God commendeth His love toward us, in that, while we were yet sinners, Christ died for us." The Greek word συνίστημι (*sunístēmi*) and translated in the KJV as "commendeth") means "to exhibit" or "to prove." Literally, it means, "to put together." At the cross God put it all together. He proved His love by the sacrifice of His Son. And, the sacrifice of His Son brought us near by His precious blood (cp. Eph. 2:13).

I remember in elementary school when I had a crush on Corrine Cunningham. I wanted her to love me. I would get a dandelion and pluck the petals, saying, "She loves me, she loves me not." If the last petal was, "She loves me," then she loved me! Well, it always came out, "She loves me." Do you know why? I rigged it! At the cross God didn't have to rig it. Every drop of our Lord's blood said, "I love you, I love you, I love you."

There is a world that needs to know God loves them sacrificially. There is a beautiful picture in Romans 3:25. There we are told that when Jesus died on the cross God "hath set [Him] forth to be a propitiation ..." The Greek word translated "set forth" is προτίθημι (*protíthēmi*) and means to expose to view. ἱλαστήριος (*hilastērios*, translated in the KJV as "propitiation") is the word in the Old Testament for mercy seat. In the Old Testament Tabernacle and Temple, the mercy seat was closed off in a cube-shaped room. There once a year the High Priest would go with blood and sprinkle it on and before the mercy seat. No one else ever saw the mercy seat but the High Priest. But, you can't keep God's love confined in a cube-shaped room; or in a church; or a Christian's life for that matter. Sooner or later it has to burst forth. When Jesus died on the cross, making the one sacrifice for sin forever (Heb. 10:12), God's love was "set forth," exposed to view so that the whole world might see.

Charles Howard was a Bible teacher at Campbell College (now University), Buies Creek, North Carolina. He also served a number of rural churches. Dr. Howard performed a wedding ceremony for a young farmer. The farm boy was unable to purchase his wife a wedding ring. "That's alright, John. If you ever get able, I would love to have a string of real pearls." John used tobacco at the time. He put his tobacco pouch in a drawer. Every time he had a craving for tobacco he would put the price of it in the pouch. Many years later Dr. Howard was invited to their home for a wedding anniversary. The wife had become an invalid. John had a wonderful country meal prepared. After supper he picked up his wife and carried her to her favorite chair in the living room. "Now close your eyes," he said. He went to his tobacco pouch and took out a string of real pearls. "Don't open your eyes until I tell you." He put the string of pearls around her neck, clasped them, then went in front of her. "Open your eyes." She opened her eyes, saw the pearls and said, "O John, are they real?" "You'd better believe it," John replied. Then she said, "O John, why did you do it?" The farmer fell on his knees, buried his head in her lap and said through tears, "Just because I love you."

When we get to heaven, see the scars in our Savior's head, His hands, His side and His feet, will we not fall at His feet and exclaim, "Oh Lord Jesus, why did you do it?" I have an idea He will say, "Just because I love you." God's love is sacrificial.

Chapter Three

GOD'S LOVE IS PERSONAL
"That whosoever believeth in Him"

§

At this point there is a different word in the Greek text from the one first translated "that" in the King James Version. This word is a subordinate conjunction meaning, in order that. The word introduces a purpose clause. What is the purpose of God sending His Son to die on the cross? To make it possible for us to be saved. This conjunction introduces a third class conditional sentence. This indicates a condition as yet undetermined, but with the prospect of determination. The glorious possibility of salvation is thus introduced in this Gospel in a nutshell.

At this point the subject of the verbs also changes. God is the subject of "loved" and "gave." Our salvation originates with God, not ourselves. Now, we are the subject of the verbs! John 3:16 gets very personal. You and I are the subject! God's love and His gift are very personal. He has you in mind!

We see in this one verse the beautiful balance we find all over the Bible. Scripture gives the Divine side and the human side of salvation. To overemphasize one to the exclusion of the other is to miss the complete message of Scripture. God's Word is far greater than any manmade systematic theology. You cannot squeeze the revelation of Scripture which reveals the infinite mind of God into any man's finite "system" of theology. To attempt to do so is to disrupt the balance between Divine sovereignty and human responsibility.

Gerald Borchert says, "God is the initiator and principal actor in salvation, and we should never think salvation originated with us. God, however, has given humanity a sense of freedom and requires us to make a choice. Accordingly, people are responsible for their believing. It is unproductive theological speculation, therefore, to minimize either the role of God or of humanity in the salvation process. The Bible and John 3:16 recognize the roles of both" (*New American Commentary*, John 1-11, Broadman Press, p. 184). More than "a sense of freedom," the sovereign God has sovereignly chosen to give man the ability to believe or not to believe.

> Scripture gives the Divine side and the human side of salvation. To overemphasize one to the exclusion of the other is to miss the complete message of Scripture.

The verb in this phrase—πιστεύω (*pisteúō*) and translated "believeth" in the KJV—is "believe." This is John's way of describing saving faith. When a person exercises saving faith they are saved. Ephesians 2:8 explains it, "For by grace are ye saved through faith; and that not of yourselves: it is the gift of God." The five words of this phrase in John 3:16 tell us what saving faith is all about.

DIMENSION

First, πάς (*pás*) is translated as "whosoever" in the English Bible and gives the dimension of saving faith. Πάς is used over 1200 times in the New Testament. Sometimes it is translated "whosoever." At other times it is translated "all" or "every." Bear with me as I get technical again. Greek grammar classifies *pás* as a pronominal substantival adjective. As an adjective it modifies the participle, "believes." As a substantival it fills the noun slot. As a pronominal it functions as a pronoun. John uses it with an article and a participle eight times in his Gospel (3:8, 15, 16, 20; 4:13; 6:40; 8:34; 18:37). The word is also used with the participle alone four times (3:15, 16; 6:40; 12:46). Here it conveys the idea of totality; the whole and every member of the whole. Kittel's says it indicates a totality and an inclusion of all individual parts (*Kittel's Theological Dictionary of the New Testament*, Gerhard Kittel, Editor. Grand Rapids: Wm. B. Eerdmans Publishing Company, vol. 5, p. 887). Colin Brown says, "Stress may be laid on each of the many individuals or parts which make up the totality" (*Dictionary of New Testament Theology*, Colin Brown, General Editor. Grand Rapids: Zondervan Publishing House, vol. 1, p. 94).

I served on the Southern Baptist Convention Peace Committee during the Conservative Resurgence. Dr. Herschel Hobbs was on the committee. He reminded us that the word *pás* is used in 2 Timothy 3:16, "All [*pás*] Scripture is inspired by God ..." Dr. Hobbs pointed out that it means the whole of Scripture and every part of Scripture is inspired of God. The same meaning is found in John 3:16, the whole world and every person in the world. As the word "world" indicates God's love for all people *collectively*, the word "whosoever" indicates His love for all people *individually*.

"Whosoever!" God unfurls a banner of invitation for the whole world. "Whosoever!" God rolls out the welcome mat of heaven to all humanity and invites all to be saved. "Whosoever" sledge hammers racial fences, dynamites social classes, bypasses gender borders and ignores restrictive theological systems. Nothing could be clearer. God exports His grace to the whole world. For those who would attempt to restrict God's love and His gift, there is a word—"Whosoever!"

Unfortunately, there have been attempts to say that the word needs no translation because the phrase "the ones believing in Him" carries all the meaning intended. However, does *pás* just mean that all who believe will be saved? If so, then the addition of this word would have been redundant. The Holy Spirit added this all-embracing adjective to emphasize there are no limits on who may believe. Dr. David Allen says, "The addition of *pás* before the participle generalizes it to every single person. The best translation is, 'Anyone who believes.' The idea is non-restrictive. Anyone, anywhere, anytime may be saved" (personal correspondence with Dr. Allen).

The fact is, *pás* has a way of showing up in passages that have to do with our salvation. Let me mention just a few:

- "He tasted death for EVERY [πάς (*pás*)] man" (Hebrews 2:9).

- "The Lord is … not willing that any should perish, but that ALL [πάς (*pás*)] should come to repentance" (2 Peter 3:9).

- "Who will have ALL [πάς (*pás*)] men to be saved, and to come unto the knowledge of the truth" (1 Timothy 2:4).

- "God, who is the Savior of ALL [πάς (*pás*)] men, specially of those that believe" (1 Timothy 4:10).

The Bible couldn't be clearer. God's desire is to make the salvation of all people possible. Consider two passages in Romans. Romans 3:22-23 says, "… for there is no difference: for ALL [πάς (*pás*)] have sinned …" All men are sinners. This is clear. Then a similar statement occurs in Romans 10:12-13, "For there is no difference between the Jew and the Greek: for the same Lord over ALL [πάς (*pás*)] is rich unto ALL [πάς (*pás*)] who call upon Him. For WHOSOEVER [πάς (*pás*)] shall call upon the name of the Lord shall be saved." *All men are savable.* Nothing could be clearer: there is no difference—all are sinners; there is no difference—all may call upon the Lord and be saved.

Who does that "all" include? You may be surprised at the answer of Scripture. Does it include false teachers? According to the Apostle Peter it does. Second Peter 2:1 mentions false prophets and teachers who would secretly bring in damnable heresies and bring upon themselves swift destruction. In the midst of that passage it says, "denying the Lord that bought them.""The Greek term translated "Lord" is δεσπότης (*despótēs*) and is used in the New Testament at times to denote a servant's subservient role to his master as in 1 Timothy 6:1, "Let as many servants as are under the yoke count their own masters [δεσπότης (*despótēs*)] worthy of all honour ..." Furthermore, even Peter uses δεσπότης (*despótēs*) to refer to human masters, "Servants, be subject to your masters [δεσπότης (*despótēs*)] with all fear ..." (1 Peter 2:18).

Consequently, some try to say δεσπότης (*despótēs*) in 2 Peter 2:1 refers to an earthly master who bought them from physical slavery, similarly to the way δεσπότης (*despótēs*) is used in the passages from Paul and Peter above. However, this makes little sense. Almost no commentators interpret "Lord" to refer to earthly masters in 2 Peter 2:1.

While it is true κύριος (*kúrios*) is the most common reference to Jesus as Lord in the New Testament (cp. Matt. 7:21-22; 9:38; 22:41-45; Mark 5:19; Luke 19:31; John 13:13; Acts 7:33; Heb. 8:2; James 4:15; *et al*), δεσπότης (*despótēs*) is often used of both God the Father and our Lord Jesus. Consider:

- Luke 2:28-29, "Then took he him up in his arms, and blessed God, and said, Lord [δεσπότης (*despótēs*)], now lettest thou thy servant depart in peace, according to thy word."

- Acts 4:24, "And when they heard that, they lifted up their voice to God with one accord, and said, Lord [δεσπότης (*despótēs*)], thou art God, which hast made heaven, and earth, and the sea, and all that in them is."

- Jude 4, "For there are certain men crept in unawares, who were before of old ordained to this condemnation, ungodly men, turning the grace of our God into lasciviousness, and denying the only Lord [δεσπότης (*despótēs*)] God, and our Lord [κύριος (*kúrios*)] Jesus Christ."

- Revelation 6:10, "And they cried with a loud voice, saying, How long, O Lord [δεσπότης (*despótēs*)], holy and true, dost thou not judge and avenge our blood on them that dwell on the earth?"

Finally, both Kittel's and BDAG indicate δεσπότης (*despótēs*) in 2 Peter 2:1 refers to the Lord Jesus Christ who bought the false teachers with His precious blood rather than earthly "masters" who bought them from the slave market. Therefore, we may be sure that πάς (*pás*) means *all* persons are savable by the grace of the Lord Jesus. Whosoever!

We might also inquire if "all" includes even Judas who betrayed our Lord. As the Lord Jesus gathered in the upper room with His disciples He said, "This cup is the new testament in my blood, which is shed for you" (Luke 22:20). The Greek word translated "you" is ὑμῶν (*humón*) and is a second person, personal *plural* pronoun, thus indicating Jesus was addressing *all* the disciples. What is more, in the very next verse He said, "But, behold, the hand of him (Judas) that betrayeth me is with me on the table" (v. 21). Judas was included in that "you" for whom His blood would be shed.

"Whosoever" includes all people everywhere. To say otherwise makes a travesty of John 3:16 and the entire message of the Bible. The love of God would be called into question. Dr.

Norman Geisler has a telling illustration: "Suppose a farmer discovers three boys drowning in his pond where he had placed signs clearly forbidding swimming. Further, noting their blatant disobedience he says to himself, 'They have violated the warning and have broken the law, and they have brought these deserved consequences on themselves.' Thus far he is manifesting his sense of justice. But if the farmer proceeds to say, 'I will make no attempt to rescue them' we would immediately perceive that something is lacking in his love. And suppose by some inexplicable whim he should declare: 'Even though the boys are drowning as a consequence of their disobedience, nonetheless, out of the goodness of my heart I will save one of them and let the other two drown. In such a case we would surely consider his love to be partial and imperfect." Then Dr. Geisler says, "Certainly this is not the picture of the God of the Bible ..." (Norman Geisler, *Chosen But Free*, second edition. Minneapolis: Bethany House Publishers, p. 50). What kind of God would not make salvation possible for all?

The whole matter of the meaning of "whosoever" goes back to the love of God. What kind of God do we have? Does He love every single person in the whole world? I believe He does. Did Christ die for every single person in the whole world? I believe He did. May any person in the whole world be saved? I believe they may! We are Biblically correct to say—God loves *whosoever*; Christ died for *whosoever* and provided redemption for *whosoever*; He calls upon *whosoever* and invites *whosoever*; God commands repentance and faith of *whosoever* and offers salvation for *whosoever*! To say otherwise is to question how we could really give a free offer of the Gospel to everyone. How could we stand in a pulpit or sit in a home and say to "whosoever" is before us that they may be saved, if no provision is made for them in the atonement? To offer something that was not provided for all is like offering a hungry person a donut hole.

I imagine sometimes that the Lord Jesus after His resurrection said, "Go find the man who made the cross and tell him, 'Whosoever'; find the man who made the crown of thorns and tell him, 'Whosoever'; find the man who drove the nails into my hands and say, 'Whosoever'; tell the men who gambled for my garments, 'Whosoever'." And so we may today say that God's love reaches "whosoever."

God's love reaches out to the old man, tottering on his cane to a Christless grave. His love reaches out to the young man, just beginning his life. His love reaches out to the business man, with full pockets and empty heart. God's love reaches out to the single mother, struggling to raise her little ones. J. Sidlow Baxter tells of a little boy who was asked, "What does 'whosoever' mean?" The boy replied, " 'Whosoever' means everybody else and me, too!"

I am glad John 3:16 says "whosoever" rather than saying, Jerry Vines. As insecure as I am, I would probably think it was a case of mistaken identity. A number of years ago I received a notice from the city of Rome, Georgia's Water Department that they were cutting off my water because I hadn't paid my bill. That was rather surprising to me because I had my own well and didn't use city water! I later found that there was another man in the city named Jerry Vines, and the rascal hadn't paid his water bill! There can be no mistaken identity when it comes to God's offer of salvation.

Make this verse a blank check and sign your name to it. Go to the remotest jungles of Africa and say to anyone you meet, "Whosoever." Travel to the snowcapped North Pole and say to anyone there, "Whosoever." Go to the finest mansion in your city and tell the people there, "Whosoever." Look for the poorest apartment in your city and tell those who live there, "Whosoever."

John "Bull" Bramlett is a friend of mine. He was known as the meanest man in the NFL. This All-Pro linebacker for the Denver Broncos was a fighter, a gambler, a drinker and a carouser. His wife came to Christ through the ministry of Bellevue Baptist Church in Memphis, Tennessee. She immediately began to pray for John to be saved. One night two men from Bellevue came to visit John. They shared the Gospel, but John was unmoved. In closing they said, "John, do you know why we came to see you tonight? It's because we love you." John was stunned. He had never had another man tell him he loved him. The next day John went to his office. He told his secretary, "Take all calls today, I want no interruptions." He closed himself in his office and began to read the New Testament. Sometime later he came to John 3:16. He read, "For God so loved the world, that He gave His only begotten Son, that whosoever ..." He stopped. "Whosoever? That could be me!" John got down on His knees, received Christ as his personal Savior and the meanest man in the NFL was saved!

DEFINITION

Let's move to the participle translated "believeth" in the English Bible. The Greek word is πιστεύω (*pisteúō*, which comes from *pístis*, the word for "faith" in the New Testament). We learn from it the definition of saving faith. The question surely arises: If God wants all people to be saved, then why aren't they? First Timothy 2:4 says, "[God] Who will have ALL [πάς (*pás*)] men to be saved, and to come unto the knowledge of the truth. Then in 1 Timothy 4:10 is written, "… God, Who is the Savior of ALL [πάς (*pás*)] men, specially of those that believe."

Scripture here adds an additional element. Those who believe are "specially" saved. The Greek word is μάλιστα (*málista*) and could be rendered "very, very much," "mostly," or "chiefly." Many translations have "especially." Though Christ's death on the cross is *sufficient* for all men, it is *efficient* only for those who believe. Salvation has been provided for all, but must be received by faith. Scripture says that salvation will only be applied to those who repent and believe.

In 2 Corinthians 5:18-21 we are taught that, "God was in Christ, reconciling the world unto Himself" (v. 19). OBJECTIVELY, He is now able and willing for anyone and everyone to be reconciled to Him. But SUBJECTIVELY, reconciliation includes human responsibility. Thus Paul says, "Be ye reconciled to God" (v. 20). Salvation becomes yours "especially" when you exercise faith in Christ.

This is vividly illustrated by the Old Testament Passover event (Exodus 12:6-7, 21-22). The night when the death angel passed over, the blood was SHED when the lamb was slain. The blood was shed for *all*. The blood was applied when it was SPRINKLED. The blood of the slain lamb only became effective when it was applied to the doorpost. Only those who were inside where the blood had been sprinkled were passed over by the death angel.

There are two categories of people in the world: those who believe and those who do not believe. Jesus said, "O Jerusalem, Jerusalem, thou that killest the prophets, and stonest them which are sent unto thee, how often WOULD I have gathered thy children together, even as a hen gathereth her chickens under her wings, and YE WOULD NOT!"(Matt. 23:37). And again, "And ye WILL NOT come to me, that ye might have life."(John 5:40).

The Greek participle literally translated is "The one believing" needs to be defined. I will get a little technical

> **Salvation has been provided for all, but must be received by faith.**

again. The participle is a present active masculine singular participle. Greek grammarians classify it as a substantival adjectival participle. Probably it is a gnomic present participle, which indicates something that is true for all without respect to time. In short, this is a statement of a general, timeless fact. The word indicates saving faith. John uses this word as indicating belief 96 times in his Gospel, nine times in chapter 3 alone. Probably the best word for today's understanding is "trust." So we translate, "Whosoever places his/her trust in Him."

To grasp the meaning of saving faith, three basic ideas must be considered. First, there is the MENTAL aspect: this is *confidence* in the Lord Jesus Christ. We trust that all He claims is true. This is the purpose for John's Gospel, "These are written, that ye might believe that Jesus is the Christ, the Son of God: and that believing ye might have life through His name" (John 20:31).

Today the trust level is low. Many of our politicians can't be trusted. We are wary about placing our future in their hands. Even some religious leaders can't be trusted. They have proven themselves unworthy of our trust. But Jesus is totally trustworthy! There is not a trace of evidence from His life or His words that He is untrustworthy.

Note that saving faith is not just believing facts about Jesus. The demons believe and tremble (James 2:19). Agrippa believed about Him, but was not saved (Acts 26:27). Saving faith is believing IN Him (see v. 15).

Second, there is the EMOTIONAL aspect of saving faith: this is *commitment* to the Lord Jesus Christ. The level of commitment today is very low. In our churches people are reluctant to make commitments. But, saving faith means we commit our life to the Lord Jesus. Some have used faith as an acrostic:

Forsaking

All

I

Take

Him.

Third, there is the VOLITIONAL aspect of saving faith: this is *choosing* the Lord Jesus and *consenting* to His Lordship. Not only is there *belief about* the Lord Jesus and *belief in* the Lord Jesus, there also is *belief toward* the Lord Jesus. More about this later.

How does this saving faith come about? The Bible seems to indicate that God has given us a faculty of faith and the will to exercise it. Romans 12:3 says, "… God hath dealt to every man the measure of faith." Though the context indicates the reference is primarily to believers, I believe it is true that all people have a capacity for faith or trust. We exercise the faculty of faith every day of our lives. You eat meals in restaurants, trusting the cook hasn't inserted poison! You deposit money in a bank, trusting the bankers are trustworthy. You board an airplane, believing the pilot is capable and responsible to fly you safely. This gift to exercise faith given from God was *effaced* by the fall, but not *erased; limited,* but not *lost; damaged,* but not *destroyed* (Geisler, *Ibid.,* p. 33).

When the Philippian jailer inquired of Paul, "Sirs, what must I do to be saved?" Paul replied, "Believe on the Lord Jesus Christ and thou shalt be saved" (Acts 16:30-31). Note that Paul made no attempt to tell the jailer he didn't have to "do" anything to be saved. We know, of course, that he didn't. Jesus had already done the work by His death on the cross. When Jesus cried, "It is finished," the work was done. That's the *Godward* side of salvation. Paul simply said, "Believe …" That's the *manward* side of salvation. And, it is a command. God commands us to repent and believe (cp. Acts 17:30). The tense of the verb is imperative. Would it not be unreasonable, even cruel, to command someone to do something they could not do? Would it not be like telling a legless man to run? Or, to ask an armless man to embrace you? Note in several verses in John 3 that saving faith may or may not be exercised (John 3:12, 18, 26).

When it comes to saving faith our faculty of faith is raised to a new level by the convicting power of the Holy Spirit (John 16:8). Second Thessalonians 2:13 says, "… God hath from the beginning chosen you to salvation through sanctification of the Spirit and belief of the truth." In salvation the Great Sheriff arrests us ("sanctification of the Spirit") and brings us to the feet of Jesus in saving faith ("belief of the truth"). Holy Spirit conviction renders a sinner capable of believing on the Lord Jesus Christ to the saving of his soul.

In John 16:8, Jesus told His disciples that when the Holy Spirit came, He would "reprove the world of sin, and of righteousness, and of judgment." The Greek word translated "reprove" in the English Bible is ἐλέγχω (*elégchō*) and means "to convict" or "refute." According to Kittel's, it indicates to "show someone his sin and to summon him to repentance" (Ibid, p. 474). Thus, through His convicting power, the Holy Spirit *enables* a person to believe. And, as we already noted above, the Lord Jesus says the reason people do not believe is that "ye WILL NOT come to me, that ye might have life" (John 5:40).

To say that man has the ability to exercise saving faith does no violence to the sovereignty of God. I repeat what I said earlier: *our sovereign God has sovereignly chosen to give to man the ability to exercise saving faith.* This is especially so when we consider the Holy Spirit's role in convicting men and women of their sin.

Notice also that "believing" precedes "everlasting life" in John 3:16. There are some who say that regeneration (being born again or receiving spiritual life) precedes faith.

They believe this is a logical conclusion from the view that unsaved people are spiritually dead and incapable of exercising faith until they are regenerated. They point to the picture of the believer being "dead in trespasses and sins" as Ephesians 2:1 indicates. They reason that, since physically dead persons are incapable of doing anything, spiritually dead persons must be made alive, before he or she can believe. Well, if dead sinners can't believe, they can't sin either. This is taking a Bible analogy too far. In Ephesians 2, those who are dead in trespasses and sins (v. 1) can "walk" (v. 2). To say regeneration precedes faith leads to a strange picture: a regenerated unbeliever!

To take such a view may be a logical extension of a manmade theological system, but no such conclusion is found in Scripture. Everywhere Scripture indicates that *after* the sinner believes, *then* he or she is born again; that is, *regenerated before receiving eternal life.*

John makes this clear in many other places in his Gospel:

- "But as many as received him, to them he gave power to become the sons of God, even to them that believe on his name" (1:12).

- "That whosoever believeth in him should not perish, but have eternal life"(3:15). "He that believeth on the Son hath everlasting life …" (3:36).

- "… He that heareth my word, and believeth on him that sent me, hath everlasting life …" (5:24).

- "... that every one which ... believeth on him, may have everlasting life" (6:40).

- "He that believeth on me hath everlasting life" (6:47).

- "But these are written, that ye might believe that Jesus is the Christ, the Son of God; and that believing ye might have life through his name" (20:31).

The order is always the same in John and throughout the New Testament: faith always *precedes* eternal life; faith *precedes* regeneration.

DIRECTION

Note the direction toward which the believer's faith is aimed. The beautiful Greek phrase is εἰς αὐτός (*eis autos*) teaching us that God's love culminates movingly, "in Him." This is the destination of saving faith. When people put their faith in the Lord Jesus Christ they are saved. Saving faith gets you to Him. And He gets you to heaven! "In Him" sounds so exclusive doesn't it? Our day of pluralism says there are many ways to heaven. All religions are equally good, we are told.

Some suggest getting to heaven is like getting to New York City. There are many airlines and many flights that will get you to New York City. But, we aren't talking about going to NYC; we're talking about going to heaven! Jesus says, "I am the way ... no man cometh to the Father, but by me."(John 14:6). Acts 4:12, says, "Neither is there salvation in any other; for there is none other name under heaven given among men, whereby we must be saved"(Acts 4:12).

The preposition εἰς (*eis*) might be translated "into Him." This carries the idea of movement toward a person and thus indicates the volitional aspect of saving faith. Consider also there exists the danger of misplaced faith. The object of our faith saves, not our faith itself. Faith in our works, our good life, our church membership, our baptism is insufficient. *Only Jesus saves.* A doctor comes to a dying girl. He tells her, "I have the skill and medicinal means to cure you. Will you let me?" She does and she is cured. Who did it? The doctor did. Who gets the glory for it? The doctor does. She just trusted "into" him to do it.

Continuing with our discussion from above, the Greek participle πιστεύω (*pisteúō*) translated "believeth" is present tense. Salvation brings us into a continuing relationship with a living Person, the Lord Jesus Christ. John explains this continuing communion the believer may have with Christ by several figures of speech. We "abide" in Christ like branches in the vine (John 15:1ff). Μένω (*ménō*, translated "abide" and used no less than eight times in this passage) means "to remain" or "to dwell." We "enter in" like sheep in a fold (John 10:1ff). When I trust in Him, I am in Him and He is in me; I love Him and He loves me!

Paul's favorite phrase for the Christian life is ἐν Χριστός (*en Christós*, translated as "in Christ" in the English Bible; cp. Rom. 3:24; 8:1-2; 12:25; 16:3; 1 Cor. 1:2; 3:1; 2 Cor. 1:21; 5:17; Gal 1:22; 6:15; Eph. 1:1; 2:6; 3:6; Phil. 1:1; 2:1; *et. al*). Israel was brought "out" that they might be brought "in." Just so when we believe "into Him" we are brought out of sin and brought into Him.

The context of John 3:16 is indicated by γάρ (gár), the coordinating conjunction at the beginning of the verse translated "For." γάρ (*gár*) links to the interview of Nicodemus with Jesus and especially the previous comments in 3:14-15. Incidentally, there is good reason to believe the conversation between Jesus and Nicodemus ends at 3:15, and John's commentary on the narrative begins in 3:16. First, Jesus never refers to Himself as "the only begotten." And second, because of the tense of the verbs, it seems to indicate the conversation was past and thus John was elaborating upon it. This is the immediate context of John 3:16. The wider context of John's Gospel has as its purpose what he expresses in John 20:31, "But these are written, that ye might believe that Jesus is the Christ, the Son of God; and that believing ye might have life through His name." Some say the context of John 3:16 indicates that Christ not only died for the elect Jews, but also the whole world of the elect Gentiles. But this view is uncommon, and few, if any, reputable commentators hold to it.

In response to Nicodemus' question as to "how" he might be born again, the beautiful illustration from Numbers 21 is used. The children murmured against God in the wilderness. As a result they were bitten by fiery snakes. In the *Septuagint* (the Greek version of the Old Testament, LXX), our little word for "all" shows up. According to it, ALL who were bitten could look to the brazen serpent Moses placed upon a pole. And EVERYONE (Numbers 21:8), ANY MAN (Numbers 21:9) who looked would live.

I have imagined something like this may have happened. A man is working in the field. He reaches for a weed, and a serpent bites him! A little boy chases his ball in the tall grass, and a serpent strikes him! A little girl reaches for a flower, and a serpent sinks its fangs into her. They are all dying in their tent. The mother goes to hear Moses speak. She rushes home. "Oh husband, I have some good news. You don't have to die. Pastor Moses says God had him put a brazen serpent on a pole. All who will look unto it will be cured, will live!"

"Woman, can't you see I'm dying? None of that religion for me. Let me die in peace." And he dies. She goes to her son and repeats the same message. "Mother," he replies, "I am university trained. I know nothing as absurd as a snake on a pole can cure me. There's no hope for me." And he dies. She then goes to her dying daughter and gives her the same message. "O mother, is it true? Can I really be healed from this snakebite?" "Yes, my dear, it is so; people all over the camp are being healed. Anyone. All. Whosoever will look will live." The girl struggles to the entrance of the tent, looks trustingly toward the brazen serpent on the pole, and she lives! The gift of life is hers personally. God's love is personal.

Chapter Four

GOD'S LOVE IS ETERNAL
"Should not perish, but have everlasting life"

§

EVERLASTING

So vast is John 3:16 it begins and ends in eternity. Beginning with God, Who has no beginning and end, the verse concludes with a life which has no ending. Eternity! The Bible speaks much of eternity. We are told of God who is eternal (Deut. 33:27). The salvation He gives is eternal (John 10:28). Even you and I are eternal (Eccl. 3:11 NASB). A little boy was asked in Sunday School to define eternity. He responded, "Sumpin' that won't quit!" An anonymous poet captured the Biblical notion of eternity:

> *"Eternity! Eternity! How long art thou, eternity?*
> *A little bird with fretting beak*
> *Might wear to naught the loftiest peak,*
> *Though but each thousand years it came;*
> *Yet thou were then as now the same,*
> *Ponder, O man, Eternity"*

There was a time when you were not; there will never be a time when you will not be. When Washington prayed at Valley

Forge, you were not. When Columbus sailed to America, you were not. When time began, you were not. When God created the universe, you were not. But, when your life on earth is ended, you will still be. When time is no more, you will be. When the stars fall from the sky, you will be. When the sun ceases to shine, you will be. When the earth stops rotating on its axis, you shall be. The big question is: Where will you be?

Eternity is indicated by the Greek word αἰώνιος (*aiōnios*, translated "everlasting" in the KJV). Two ideas are indicated in the Greek. First is the *quantitative* idea. αἰώνιος (*aiōnios*) indicates something that is endless or never ending, and thus not affected by time. We may live each day by our wristwatch, but no time pieces exist in Heaven! The second is the *qualitative* idea, indicating something that is different in quality. This is especially meaningful when it is joined with the word "life," which we will consider later. John 3:16 concludes with only two possible eternal destinies. All people are heading to one of two eternal existences: either we will be in the land of eternal perishing or the land of eternal living. God loves every person and wants them to escape eternal perishing and experience eternal living.

PERISHING

God's love rescues people from eternal hell. The Greek phrase is μή ἀπόλλυμι (*mē apóllumi*, translated "should not perish" in KJV). μή (*mē*) is a negative particle and thus translated "not." It further implies something does not exist. ἀπόλλυμι (*apóllumi*) means "to utterly destroy"—destroy not in the sense of *eradication*. As we learned above, we all exist forever either in the land of eternal perishing or the land of eternal living. Rather, *apóllumi* means to destroy in the sense of *ruination*. Hence, for the believer, *to perish does not exist*. But for the unbeliever, μή ἀπόλλυμι (*mē apóllumi*) implies a non-ending, catastrophic future.

Perish! The word is a noxious weed growing in this fresh garden of love. Perish! The word is a discordant note in this symphony of love. Stop! You can smell fire burning. Look! You can see worms crawling. Listen! You can hear weeping and gnashing of teeth. All hell *itself* is in that word.

In addition, the Greek word translated "perish" is an aorist middle subjunctive, indicating a condition as yet unfulfilled, but the possibility of fulfillment is there. Again, the word does not mean annihilation or the end of existence. Rather, the idea is not *destruction* but *devastation*. It means to be *ruined*. Luke 15 uses the word 8 times, with the meaning of "lost." Sometimes the word indicates physical destruction. In Matthew 8:25 the disciples on the sea cried, "Lord, save us, we perish [ἀπόλλυμι (*apóllumi*)]." The word also is used to indicate a spiritual condition. Kittel says that it speaks of "… an eternal plunge into Hades and a hopeless destiny of death … an everlasting state of torment and death" (Kittel, Ibid., vol. 1, p. 394). "Perish" indicates the final tragedy of a soul.

The concept of hell is perfectly logical. In one of my rural churches there was no garbage service. So, when our cans were full I would take them to the county garbage dump. As I approached I could smell the stench. When I arrived, I saw the fires burning and the scavenger birds and dogs rummaging through the piles of garbage. Jesus referred to hell by use of a word that was used to refer to the garbage dump of Jerusalem. For example, Jesus said in Mark 9, "it is better for thee to enter into life maimed, than having two hands to go into hell [γέεννα (*géenna*)], into the fire that never shall be quenched" (v. 43; cp. vv. 45, 47). γέεννα (*géenna*) is found twelve times in the New Testament and Jesus uses it eleven of the twelve times. Hell is the garbage dump of the universe.

Several years ago I was having lunch with an unsaved billionaire in Jacksonville. In the midst of the lunch my friend blurted out, "Do you believe there is a hell?" My immediate reply was, "Of course I do. If there wasn't one, I'd give $5 to start one." He looked at me in stunned disbelief. I continued, "Would you want to be in heaven with the Hitlers and Mussolinis and Saddam Husseins? If they were in heaven, they would ruin it. There has to be a place like hell for people like them." Every time we see a garbage can or garbage truck, they preach us a sermon on hell.

Hell is also the insane asylum of the universe. When I was a student at Mercer University I took a course in psychology. One of our areas of interest was insanity. We took a field trip to the state mental hospital in Milledgeville, Georgia. As we were walking on the grounds we heard a blood curdling scream." What is that?' one of the students asked. Our guide replied, "That's someone in the ward for the criminally insane. They are locked up in padded cells. If they got out, they would kill as many people as they could." Think about it.

Jesus had the tenderest heart that ever beat in a human breast. He said more about hell than any person in the Bible. Someone has said that 13% of all His teaching was about judgment or hell. Is not a person spiritually insane to reject God's gracious offer of salvation provided by the death of His only begotten Son?

One of my mentors was Evangelist Jess Hendley. He preached on the reality of hell with such power and fervor that some referred to him as "hell fire and damnation Hendley." We were having lunch on an occasion and one of the local pastors walked up to our table. "Well, if it isn't hell fire and damnation Hendley." I saw the hurt on Dr. Hendley's face. After the pastor left, Jess said to me, "You see, Jerry, I really do believe that there is a hell and I don't want anyone to go there." If we really believe there is a hell, shouldn't we earnestly desire that no one go there?

What is more, the word translated "perish" in John 3:16 is in the aorist tense, indicating the total, all inclusive, final tragedy of a soul. In other places "perish" is in the present tense. First Corinthians 1:18 uses the present tense, so that the phrase might be translated, "them that are in the process of perishing." I repeat: all people are in one of two sides of existence—perishing or living.

Putting 1 Corinthians 1:18 and John 3:16 together we get the picture. The onset of the perishing begins now, but the culmination of the perishing is in eternity. Sometimes people declare, "I believe all the hell you will ever get is what you experience on this earth." If you are saved, that is true. All the "hell" believers will ever know is what they experience in this world. But, if you are lost and refuse to receive Christ as your Savior, your "hell" begins here and continues forever.

While the use of the present tense is in some places in the New Testament, the aorist in John 3:16 suggests a condition that begins here and now, but does not reach full and terrible culmination until the final condemnation. Dr. Bill Hull says the translation might well be, "should not come to a dead end with everything utterly lost."(William E. Hull, *Love In Four Dimensions*. Nashville: Broadman Press, p. 68). A bright shiny new car soon shows a little spot of rust (called car cancer by dealers). Next the tires get worn. The car is in the process of perishing. Sooner or later the car is in a junk yard, windows smashed and the inside in shambles. The onset of the car's "perishing" culminates when the car is hauled to the junk yard.

The same Greek word used to describe eternal life is also used to describe eternal hell. Jesus said, "These shall go away into everlasting [αἰώνιος (*aiốnios*)] punishment: but the righteous into life eternal [αἰώνιος (*aiốnios*)]" (Matt. 25:46). What an awesome thought. In hell for eternity. Once in hell, always in hell. Can you imagine a person going into hell, knowing there will never be a return? People don't go to hell for a weekend visit to see how they like it. *Once in hell, always in hell.*

In hell to cry, "It's hot! Give me some air." No air in hell. " In hell to ask, "I'm thirsty. Give me a drink of water." No water in hell. In hell to shout, "It's dark in here. Turn on a light." No light in hell. In hell to beg, "I don't want to live in here. Let me die." No death in hell. Forever in hell! The chains of hell are engraved, "Forever!" The flames of hell sizzle, "Forever!" The demons hiss, "Forever!"

There are those who object to the concept of hell, eternal perishing. "How," they ask, "can a loving God send people to hell?" He doesn't. People who go to hell volunteer to go there. Jesus made it very clear that everlasting fire is "prepared for the devil and his angels" (Matthew 25:41). C. S. Lewis said there are two kinds of people: Those who say to God, "Thy will be done"; and those to whom God will say, "thy will be done."

If you go to hell, you go without an invitation. I can imagine the Lord Jesus saying to those who go away into hell, "I didn't mean for you to go there. I died on the cross so you wouldn't have to go there. I endured hell for you so you wouldn't have to endure it."

LIVING

The Greek conjunction ἀλλά (*allá*) is universally translated as "but." This little word introduces a breathtaking reversal in potential and possibility. The Greek word is an adversative conjunction, denoting a contrast. Coiled up in a tiny, one syllable word rests the hinge of our hope. What a change in thought! This little word carries us from agony to ecstasy; from misery to glory; from hell to heaven.

God's love reaches to eternal heaven. ἔχω (*echo*, translated "have" in the KJV) is a present active subjunctive. The verb is a subjunctive, indicating a condition as yet unfulfilled, but with a glorious possibility. Note that the verb changes from "perish," a verb in the aorist tense to "have," a verb in the present tense. The idea is something that can continue to be enjoyed forever and forever. The believer possesses and enjoys everlasting life.

Let's look carefully at the phrase translated "everlasting life." The Greek phrase is ζωή αἰώνιος (*zōế aiốnios*)—"life eternal." *zōế* usually refers to physical life and contrasts to death and nonexistence. It also refers to life without end. Says the writer to the Hebrews when explaining the Melchisedec priesthood of Jesus, "Who is made, not after the law of a carnal commandment, but after the power of an endless life [ζωή ἀκατάλυτος (*zōế akatálutos*)]" (7:16). ἀκατάλυτος (*akatálutos*, translated "endless") literally means "without dissolving" or as some put it, "indissoluble." When the Old Testament priests offered animal sacrifices, the animals ceased to exist. Contrarily, when Jesus offered Himself once for all as a sacrifice for sin (cp. Hebrews 9:26), He did not cease to exist. Believers too have the power of an endless life.

Stop! Consider these two words. Look! And you will see gates of pearl, streets of gold and a river and tree of life. Listen! And you will hear anthems of angels and songs of saints. All heaven is in that phrase.

Additionally, the phrase "everlasting life" occurs 17 times in John's Gospel. In the New Testament "life" is used to describe three kinds of life: physical; spiritual; and eternal. "Everlasting" (*aiŏnios*) has two basic ideas. Quantitatively, it indicates a *time* element. The time indicated is of endless duration. Qualitatively, it indicates *superior* in quality. When a person believes on the Lord Jesus, God gives the gift of eternal life (cp. John 17:3 and 1 John 5:11-13). At the moment you receive Christ your eternal destiny changes.

A careful study of eternal life in the New Testament yields two notions. First, eternal life is a *present* possession. First John 5:12 expresses it, "He that hath the Son hath (right here and now) life …" The Lord Jesus, Who is life (cp. John 14:6), gives us life, a different quality of life right now!

Second, eternal life is a *future* expectation. Eternal life is a present possession and also a future promise. First John 2:25 says, "And this is the promise that He hath promised us, even eternal life." This future expectation is our hope ("… according to the hope of eternal life" Titus 3:7). So, "everlasting life" is a

Person and a place. When you are saved you get Jesus now and heaven some day!

Just think about it. *Once in heaven, always in heaven!* Heaven will be heaven because of the absence of some things. No tears and no sorrow; no pain and no death; no curse and no sin. Heaven will be heaven because of the presence of some things. We will see our loved ones again. I am looking forward to seeing my father and mother again. We will see friends again. I look forward to seeing Milton Graves, Adrian Rogers, Wayne Hamrick, Jerry Falwell, and countless others again.

Imagine stepping through the gates into heaven and hearing the words, "Welcome to heaven!" We will see Jesus. To me, the one most beautiful word in the Bible is, "Jesus" (Philippians 2:10). The two most beautiful words in the Bible are: "Jesus wept" (John 11:35). The three most beautiful words in the Bible are: "God is love" (1 John 4:8). The four most beautiful words in the Bible are: "Christ died for us" (1 Cor. 15:3). The five most beautiful words in the Bible are: "They shall see His face" (Rev. 22:4).

> **Eternal life is a present possession and also a future promise.**

What will it be like when we see Jesus? The old Gospel song has this line, *O, I want to see Him, look upon His face ...* Another one says, *One glimpse of His dear face, all sorrow will erase.* I look forward to being able to kneel at His feet and thank Jesus for loving me enough to die on the cross for me. And I'll be able to do it for all eternity!

CONCLUSION

I have just touched the hem of the garment of this marvelous John 3:16. Let me conclude by telling a story I once heard. I cannot vouch for its authenticity, but it does convey the tremendous power of John 3:16.

As the story goes, there was a young newspaper boy selling papers on the streets of a northern city. The weather was cold, snow was falling, and the ground was frozen. The paper boy approached a police officer and said, "Excuse me sir, but you wouldn't know where a poor, cold boy could find a warm place to sleep tonight would you?" The policeman was a Christian. He said to the boy, "Son, right down the street there is a big white house. Go to the house and knock on the door. When they come to the door just say, 'John 3:16' and they will let you in." The boy went to the house, knocked on the door. A man opened the door and the boy said, "John 3:16." "Come in, son," the man said.

The little boy entered, saw the vastness of the room and said, "I don't know what John 3:16 is, but it sure will get a little boy into a big house."

"Are you cold?" asked the man. "Sir, so cold I can't stop shaking." The man took him to a big fire place. As the boy warmed himself he said, "I don't understand what John 3:16 is all about, but it will sure get a cold little boy warm."

"Are you hungry, son?" "O sir, I haven't had a good meal in days." He was taken to a table laden with good food, and ate to his heart's content. "This John 3:16 will sure make a hungry boy full."

Could you use a bath?" inquired the man. "I haven't had a bath in a few days." The man carried him upstairs to a shiny bathtub, filled it with warm water, and gave him some soap and a towel. As the little boy enjoyed the warm bath he exclaimed, "I don't know what John 3:16 means, but it sure will get a dirty boy clean."

Then the man asked, "Are you tired?" "I haven't had a good night's sleep in days, sir." He was carried by the man to a large bed with a soft mattress and plenty of cover. "Son, climb in there and sleep as long as you like." The little boy, dozing off said, "I don't understand John 3:16, but it will rest a tired boy."

He woke up the next morning and the man who led the mission used John 3:16 to bring the boy to Christ and eternal life.

Do you want to go to God's Big House? John 3:16. Are you cold from this world's freezing winds? John 3:16. Are you tired of this world's junk food and hungry for something to satisfy? John 3:16. Are you stained and blemished and spotted by the sin of the world and want to be clean? John 3:16. Are you weary in soul and want rest? John 3:16! Whosoever!

Bibliography

Allen, David L. and Steve W. Lemke. Whosoever Will: A Biblical-Theological Critique of Five-Point Calvinism. Nashville: B&H Academic, 2101.

Arndt, William, Frederick W. Danker and Walter Bauer. A Greek-English Lexicon of the New Testament and Other Early Christian Literature. 3rd Edition. Chicago: Unioversity of Chicago Press, 2000.

Borchert, Gerald L. John 1-11. Nashville: B&H Publishing Group, 1996.

Brown, Colin. The New International Dictionary of New Testament Theology. Zondervon, 1981.

Dawkins, Richard. The God Delusion. Great Britan: Batam Books, 2006.

Geisler, Norman L. Chosen But Free: A Balanced View of God's Sovereignty and Free Will. Grand Rapids: Bethany House Publishers, 2010.

Gerhard Kittel, Gerhard Friedrich. Theological Dictionary of the New Testament. 10th. 10 vols. Eerdmans Publishing Company, 1977.

Hitchens, Christopher. God is not Great. New York: Warner Twelve, 2007.

Hull, William E. Love in four dimensions. Nashville: Broadman Press, 1982.

Joseph Henry Thayer, Carl Ludwig Wilibald Grimm, Christian Gottlob Wilke. Thayer's Greek-English lexicon of the New Testament: coded with the numbering system from Strong's exhaustive concordance of the Bible. Hendrickson, 1996.

MacArthur, John. NKJV MacArthur Study Bible. Nashville: Thomas Nelson, 2010.

Roberrtson, Archibald Thomas. Word Pictures in the New Testament. Vol. V. Nashville: Broadman Press, 1932.

Tozer, A. W. Christ the Eternal Son. Christian Publications, 1982.

More Resources by Jerry Vines

Jerry Vines Ministries

2295 Towne Lake Parkway

Suite 116 #249

Woodstock, Georgia 30189

I hope WHOSOEVER has blessed the reader as much as it blessed the author! God has wonderfully blessed the preaching of His Word through the years by adding to His church those whom He graciously saved (Acts 13:48). Remaining faithful to His Word has remained my heartbeat for over a half century in pastoral ministry.

Below are more resources you might find equally as helpful. If you find something of interest, all resources are available at www. jerryvines.com.

Books

All the Days: Daily Devotions For Busy Believers (Free Church Press, 2012) is a daily devotional I wrote with busy believers in mind. A biblical text and brief inspirational commentary is available for each day of the week for an entire year. I alternate monthly between Old and New Testaments. Here's a sample entry for August 27:

> *"...for God loveth a cheerful giver."*
> *2 Corinthians 9:7*

Again today we read about the matter of giving. God is interested in what you give; He is more interested in how you give. We should give with several attitudes. READINESS (vv. 1-5). We must be ready to give as we have committed. Perhaps you have committed yourself to give to your church. Be ready to do it. BOUNTIFULNESS (vv. 6, 8-11). Like the laws of sowing and reaping, giving involves God's abundant blessings upon us. This doesn't mean you will be rich if you give. It means you will have your needs met and have spiritual blessings in your life. CHEERFULNESS (v. 7). The word, "cheerful," literally means hilarious. God doesn't want sad givers, mad givers, but glad givers. THANKFULNESS (vv. 12-15). Giving is a part of worship. When we get and when we give we should be thankful.

Prayer: "Lord, today I will become a happy giver."

A Journey Through the Bible: From Genesis to Malachi, Volume I, (Free Church Press, 2011). The study includes a brief introduction to each of the 39 books. In addition, every book of the Old Testament is outlined in easy to remember format.

A Journey Through the Bible: From Matthew to Revelation, Volume II (Free Church Press, 2011). The study includes a brief introduction to each of the 27 books. In addition, every book of the New Testament is outlined in easy to remember format.

Other book titles include:

The Genesis Account of Creation
Studies on the truth about creation and evolution.

God's Perfect 10
Sermons on the 10 Commandments

Immortal Kombat
Sermons on the book of Job

It Happened At Bethlehem
The Birth of Jesus Christ from the Old Testament
perspective of the book of Ruth.

Matthew & Mark Sermon Outlines
Over 100 sermon outlines

People Who Met Jesus
From a prostitute to a preacher, from a young man to a
dying thief, studies of those who were changed by Christ

*Power in the Pulpit — How to Prepare and Deliver Expository
Sermons*
Fresh ideas and inspiration for the greatest job on earth

The Corinthian Confusion
Messages from Corinthians for today's people of God

The Spirit Book
Three books in one! The life and work of the Holy Spirit.

§

In addition to books, you will find CDs and DVDs of
messages I've preached in both churches and conferences
throughout the years.

What is more, perhaps your church is considering options for
a new Bible Study curriculum. May I recommend you check

out Vines *By The Book* Bible Study series? This exciting new series takes the study group through each book of the Bible chapter by chapter. The entire New Testament is now complete, and the Old Testament is well under way. We offer a sample lesson to download. Along with the others, you will find this vital resource at www.jerryvines.com.

Books by Free Church Press
www.freechurchpress.com

A Gentle Zephyr — A Mighty Wind: Silhouettes of Life in the Spirit, by J. Gerald Harris; Foreword by Jerry Vines. Moving messages, filled with illustrations, on the Holy Spirit.

Urgent: Igniting a Passion for Jesus, by Joe Donahue; Foreword by Ergun Caner. A powerful story how God changed one man and how God used the man to help change others. Offers a clear Gospel message.

Ancient Wine and the Bible: The Case for Abstinence, by David R. Brumbelow; Foreword by Paige Patterson. Detailed study of ancient production and kinds of wine, Scripture, and reasons for abstinence.

A Journey Through the Bible: From Genesis to Malachi, Volume I, by Jerry Vines. Introduction, outline, and synopsis of each Old Testament book by one of America's leading expositors.

A Journey Through the Bible: From Matthew to Revelation, Volume II, by Jerry Vines. Introduction, outline, and synopsis of each New Testament book.

All The Days: Daily Devotions For Busy Believers by Jerry Vines. Brief, expository devotions for every day of the year. Explores different books of the Bible from both the Old and New Testaments.

Green Pastures of a Barren Land: finding contentment in life's desolate seasons by Candise Farmer. After the Foreword by Kay Arthur, Candise offers Biblical encouragement to those facing difficult moments in life. In addition, Candise offers an inductive Bible study for small groups as a supplement to her book.

Straight Shooting: Pastoral Reflections for Today's Church by William "Bill" Harrell. A veteran pastor takes an honest look at the moral corruption of our culture and the church's unfortunate failure to stop it.

Born Guilty? A Southern Baptist View of Original Sin by Adam Harwood. Dr. Harwood makes the clear biblical distinction between "imputed sinful guilt" and "inherited sinful nature" and shows why it's significant for believers today. The first booklet in an exclusive teaching series by Free Church Press.

What is Calvinism? everything you need to know about Calvinism...and then some by Peter Lumpkins. The author answers the question concerning what Calvinism is, then shows Calvinism's inadequacy as a theological system to be imposed upon Scripture. *What is Calvinism?* is a part of an exclusive teaching series by Free Church Press specifically written for those without a theological background.

Preach The Word! A Collection of Essays on Biblical Preaching in Honor of Jerry Vines, edited by David L. Allen and Peter Lumpkins. Contributors include a "Who's Who" among Southern Baptists–Paige Patterson, O.S. Hawkins, Mac Brunson, Steve Smith, Malcolm Yarnell, Stephen Rummage, Steve Lemke, Johnny Hunt, Emir and Ergun Caner among many others. This essay collection may define Biblical preaching from a Southern Baptist perspective for years to come.

CPSIA information can be obtained at www.ICGtesting.com
Printed in the USA
LVOW06s1230160913

352623LV00001B/1/P